Successful Integrated Planning For the Supply Chain

How to enhance your business with supply chain integration techniques

Andrei Besedin

© **Copyright 2019 - All rights reserved.**

The content contained within this book may not be reproduced, duplicated or transmitted without direct written permission from the author or the publisher.

Under no circumstances will any blame or legal responsibility be held against the publisher, or author, for any damages, reparation, or monetary loss due to the information contained within this book. Either directly or indirectly.

Legal Notice:

This book is copyright protected. This book is only for personal use. You cannot amend, distribute, sell, use, quote or paraphrase any part, or the content within this book, without the consent of the author or publisher.

Disclaimer Notice:

Please note the information contained within this document is for educational and entertainment purposes only. All effort has been executed to present accurate, up to date, and reliable, complete information. No warranties of any kind are declared or implied. Readers acknowledge that the author is not engaging in the rendering of legal, financial, medical or professional advice. The content within this book has been derived from various sources. Please consult a licensed professional before attempting any techniques outlined in this book.

By reading this document, the reader agrees that under no circumstances is the author responsible for any losses, direct or indirect, which are incurred as a result of the use of information contained within this document, including, but not limited to, — errors, omissions, or inaccuracies.

Table of Contents

Introduction

Chapter 1

Supply Chain Integration

    The Goal of Supply Chain Integration

    Information Flows

    Physical logistics

Chapter 2

Definition and Challenges

    Challenges and Obstacles of Supply Chain Integration

    Framework for Analysis

Chapter 3

Partnerships, Alliances, and Cooperation

Chapter 4

Strategy and Planning

    Management of customers' requests

    Logistic Management

    Operation flexibility management

    Setting up standards of trade

    Management of Purchases

    Business integration

    Application Integration

    Adaptation to the extranet system

    Business process integration

Chapter 5

Strategy Implementation

    Implementation issues

Chapter 5

Supply Chain Models

    SCOR Model

    Agile vs. Lean

Chapter 6

Elements in the Operational Management Level

    Internal Integration and Collaborative Operation of Within Focal Firm

    Organize around Outcomes and not tasks

    External Collaboration and Collaborative Supply Chain Operation

    Supplier Integration

    Distributor Integration

    Customer Integration

Conclusion

Introduction

For businesses to have an edge in this information age, every business should be in charge of the totality of their business chain. Supply chain management brings about mutualism and cooperation within the organization and working together with business partners, patrons, and suppliers.

Planning and process integration is a necessary part of supply chain management and process. This does not involve only executing the ERP system alone but also being certain they convey or assemble with previous methods. It also includes the integration of ERP and supply chain management system with CRM, e-market, product lifestyle management, and e-procurement. This makes them visible on the internet and improves the whole value chain.

In our present day, there have been a series of changes in the business world. Most organization are fast-growing, collaborating, and also continuous planning within the supply chain because of the swift growth of applied science like prevalent cordless and communication network.

The underlying logistic network is quickly changing into what is known as Supply network. This is a robust and systematic procedure where every system in which organization operates increases the importance of all supply chains.

Integration can be defined as steps of restructuring and joining component to bring about something new. Previous supply network integration, its meaning is always restricted to the boundary of the organization: combination emphasizes bringing together every organization with implementing and capable communications.

In this book, you will learn about the various concept of supply chain management and how to integrate it into your business model to achieve success. Successful supply chain integration will not be possible if you do not understand the initial problems and how best you can solve them. I hope you will find the answers to some pertinent questions about supply chain integration by reading this book. Happy reading!

Chapter 1

Supply Chain Integration

The search for new models that will help companies become more competitive is never-ending. Several strategies like Supply Chain Management (SCM), Just in Time (JIT), Theory of Constraint (TOC), and Total Quality Management (TQM) are some of the strategies to have been adopted.

Beautiful enough, they have delivered well, and have assisted in improving the production processes, reducing the cost of production, and helped businesses compete better. The basic fact about globalization and internet influence on SCM is a phenomenon to be known by every MIS researcher.

The search for improvement in competitiveness and transformation of business for the best has led many companies into studying the effect of information technology. Companies started exploring and integrating the business process with technology as the primary enabler instead of the former inefficient automating processes.

This process is what brought about the birth of the Supply Chain Management model. A typical supply chain must include all stages involved in satisfying a customer's request, and the stages may be direct or indirect.

The supply chain also contains the manufacturer, transporter, supplier, warehouse, retailers, the third party logistic, and the customer. The supply chain management is essential for maximizing overall value generated instead of the profit generated in a supply chain.

According to the American Professional Association, SCM involves the total planning and management of the entire activity of sourcing and procurement, conversion and the whole logistics management tasks.

More importantly, it means efficient collaboration and coordination or channel partners. All of these may include the suppliers, middle-men, third-party service providers, and customers.

A more renewed attention is given to the concept of customer and suppliers integrative relationship between the 1980s and 1990s. At this time, businesses improve their relationship with strategic customers (selected clients). At this time, the emphasis was more on refining the arrangements for working of suppliers.

This action led to a trend of increased collaboration between the SC, and it could be explained in the light of these three factors;

- Globalization of manufacturing processes where local markets were subjected to global standards.
- Development and operation of environmentally friendly products and services were required of the manufacturing system.
- There was increased stress to the business and organizational structure where the manufacturing system operates.

The collaboration was improved based on the desire to spread the control and coordination of all operations across the overall supply process, thereby managing the flow process by replacing the market and vertical integration.

Although the definition often focuses on the integration internal to firms and organization, yet, the importance spans beyond the firms and touches all external entities that are active in the supply chain.

With developments experienced so far in SCM, cutting cost is not only comfortable, generating new revenue and high profit is now feasible. Linking these novels methods together to achieve a competitive advantage of a seamless flow of supply chain is currently the only challenge.

The creation of collaborative outside and cross-company processes for designing products that satisfy the demands of the market can be achieved efficiently.

The four stages required for creating the supply chain include:

1. The supply chain network

2. The internal supply chain (otherwise manufacturing plants)
3. End-users, and
4. The distribution system.

The following flows move up and down the stages; material flow, service flow, information flow, and the fund flow.

The Goal of Supply Chain Integration

The goal for SCM is depicted to "erode transmission barrier and remove excesses" via coordination, tracking and managing processes. Studies also report it as trying to increase the links between every part within the chain, (to preside) the best decision and having every piece of chain work together in a better method. Thereby, making supply chain visible, and establish bottlenecks.

The primary drives for integration are;

- Vast Changes in Information
- There is a high level of competition globally developing better customer service and better markets.
- Birth of a new kind of intra-organizational connections.

The foundation for integration can be depicted by connection, trust, alliance, information sharing, shared tech, and a fundamental shift from controlling personal functional process.

The scope of integration starts with designing your products, including every step that leads to the final purchase of the item. Few people reported every activity that occurs all through the life of a product, which includes recycling, service, and reverses logistics.

The primary thing about integration is enhancing profit and competitive positioning. It also states that supply chain connotes 60-80% of a particular organizational structure, a 10% decrease can bring about 40-50% efficiency in pre-tax gains.

Progressive changes and the notion of integration changed periodically where the logistics network acts as a collective unit. It extends to a simulated organization without referring to traditional enterprise boundaries. This could be motivated expressly by the demands of the customers through the method of the electronic e-commerce website.

This direction will develop into significant modification in most organization, which will finally lead to the best use of a subcontract service provider. It is also true that the key to planning is to concentrate basically on bringing new changes in the organization and widen the scope to involve both customers and suppliers.

The principal value following usually involves decreased cycle time and cost. The essential thing concentrates on setting goals around professionals via unity and cooperation, quotes old-fashioned methods of setting goals within distribution/manufacturing professionals as an illustration of opportunities for the best alignment before advancement in SCM practices.

Supply chain network also suggests that suppliers and patrons institute appropriate partnership with the goal and likely results of the decreased index, temporal times, and the best service to customers.

Information Flows

Applying information tech for efficient integration of logistics network has intentions of decreasing multiple levels. There are two kinds of complexity namely, specification and dynamism. The **specific complexity** happens when there are most alterations required to be controlled. **Dynamism complexity** arises where the cause and effects are apart, and tedious to connect with using both space and time.

- Circumstances where cause and effects are understood and intentions periodically in terms of intervention are not distinct. Typical prediction, implementation, and theoretical methods are not prepared to confront dynamic complexity.

- "Bullwhip effect" is an illustration of a typical SCM result gotten from situations that have dynamism complexity.

This process discusses the demand steps noticed by a specific part of a logistics network tends to be more flexible as we increase our supply chain. That is to say, orders notified by the upstream region of the logistics network are more flexible than the rules noticed by the downstream parts.

Signs of this result are severe index, loss of income, inefficient production scheduling, inaccurate and final capacity planning. It also states the means to, and control of information is essential to reduce this kind of variation.

Innovatory organization in several industries have discovered it is possible to manage the bullwhip effect and advance its logistics network performance by synchronizing information and implementation alongside the supply chain.

Attributing reason for bullwhip effect varies when it was noticed at first. System behaviors can be as a result of interacting of structures (efficient enterprise configuration and information source), amplification, delays (time interval within cause and effects, and planning).

It is also observed that the underlying influence is unfounded as human behaviors obsessed by disagreement in real demand. It is also true that the issue is within the infrastructure of the logistics network, thereby establishing practices like increase in price and rationing, demand predictions update, shortage gains, and order batching as crucial drivers. When there is merging of business is vital for efficient and well-timed information, though some disagree that proper time is not a valuable solution.

Physical logistics

The following factors are enhancing the significance of physical inventory management:

- Reduced life-cycles of product

- Decreasing levels of product standardization and customization demands
- Customers needing the delivery of goods within a shorter time frame
- Increased competition level as a result of globalization and reduction of tariff barriers
- Increase in rate and number of change as well as uncertainty

Inventory level in supply chains linked directly to cycle times, while cycle times are also significantly related to distance, complexity, and uncertainty.

From the perspective of physical goods movement, an integrated supply chain will give firms the chance to compete based on flexibility and speed, while also holding minimum inventory level in the supply chain.

Instead of the goods to be kept at different points within the supply chain, it will be moved within these points. Research shows that companies that experience vast reductions in cycle times were also successful in transforming it into real business benefits.

Aside from the possibility of providing a basis for competitive advantage, a recent study also reveals that the necessary infrastructure to sustain a streamlined flow of product is far behind the fast developments experienced in information technology.

It is predicted that there will be immense pressure on global shipping infrastructures within the next three to five years as e-commerce growth takes an upward rise globally.

The critical areas of the problem identified include:

Fragmented regulatory rules

Japan is a notable example whereby its imports have up to 17,000 different trade laws, while agencies of the government solely sell certain products in China.

Inadequate intermediaries

It is projected that global shipments will need an average of 27 separate parties involved in shipment before it is completed. These include cargo space brokers, inland transport carriers, regional and country compliance intermediaries, tax officers of government agencies, etc.

Complications in costs

Unplanned changes tax and duties between countries can also affect sourcing decisions.

Distribution center and facility location decision can also affect the distribution of goods. But what are some of the primary decision consideration for the logical design of a global logistics network? They are:

- Number of distribution centers available
- Where they need to be located
- The Methods used in distribution and the capacity each should have
- The customers that each center will attend based on order and product type.

However, for incoming logistics, there are significant issues, for example, if they are rationalizing the supplier base, contemplating on which suppliers to drop and which is to be kept, also, they have to consider which supplier should supply each plant by a class of parts.

There are other general issues though, they include: relative merits of tax havens as against additional duty costs or freight, where the customers and suppliers are located, the length of the material pipeline in space and time, and the time involved in transit and the cost of various transportation options, and finally, the design of products for optimal shipping configuration.

It should be noted that there has been a significant shift from the application of technological solutions to the physical distribution system. And this includes racking systems, automated warehousing, and trucks.

The focus is moving down to information technology due to diminishing marginal returns in physical handling technologies, though it isn't noted whether these technologies are being stuck in many material-handling systems like the forklift trucks and automated materials handling systems. But does that mean that the physical side of the distribution issue isn't worthy of note or somewhat insignificant? Definitely no!

For instance, a survey conducted in the USA by A.T Kearney figured out that only 9% of those involved in the study shows that they have competency in either transport or logistic processes and undertaken.

While on the flip side, the study indicated that 90% were planning to make supply chain initiatives, and 18% from that 90% admit that by implementing IT, their supply chain was sufficiently supported.

You can notice that there is a low level of fundamental expertise in traditional logistics functions. And that means companies run the risk of seeing IT implementation as a means to tackle and address problems that are more rooted in organizational competencies. Therefore, what overall conclusion can be made?

Companies have consistently erred in paying adequate attention to areas like transport and logistics, purchasing, and distribution. More severe problems include the inability to align their IT systems and organizing their firm's supply chain needs, and the traditional nature of their relations with external suppliers and customers.

Chapter 2

Definition and Challenges

In this present age, there has been little modification in the business world, which added tremendously to the growth of logistic chain networks.

Firstly, the result of the interconnected world and the rise of a business organization operating in multiple companies, business partnership, and joint ventures, are discovered to be responsible for vital success.

Secondly, advancement in technology, specifically the unexpected fall in communication price, which is an essential part led to a modification in synchronizing amidst members of the logistic network. These might result in problems in the integration of the logistics system.

The integration of the SCM is placed under necessary debate and conversation. As enterprise search for growth of partnerships and better efficient pieces of information with countries that do business with other countries regularly.

The process internally produces interlink and extend old fashioned boundaries of an organization.

Physical implementation brings about more dependence on information tech, and this system becomes facilitators of advanced collaborated arrangements. Organizations are challenged with managing smaller enterprise as technologies results in interdependence, network of process, and shared goal.

The sincere planning of SCM has become visible for firms participating in high integration, which becomes a great advantage for them. The purpose of this article is to describe and make analysis that relates to implementing and integration of SCM practices.

As a result, it is divided into the following subgroups:

- Logistic supply network

This part discusses problems that relate to the inclusion of essential methods over enterprise boundaries via effective communication, collaboration, partnership, and coalition. It involves applying improved tech for striking pieces of information and synchronize flows of goods within trading partners.

- Implementation and Plan

SCM acts as a plan for trading matter also with factors that relates to the number of strategies needed.

- Implementation Problem

Elements that is extremely important for the successful planning, and even problems particular to intra and inter-organizational view for supply chain initiatory are all embedded in this class.

Challenges and Obstacles of Supply Chain Integration

There are numerous yet unique challenges faced by supply chain management (SCM), especially when it comes to the integration of the supply-chain strategies with the entire corporate business strategy. Due to the changing business realities with regards to globalization over the years, the supply chain is now an essential feature on the CEO's priority list.

A Supply chain is often considered in most cases when the CEO's are planning to cut costs on production or when things go wrong. This is because the supply chain is the most critical part of the organization. The efficiency of this process is necessary to optimize business-related operations.

The Multi-National Company (MNC) may benefit from global integration, if there is a differential advantage to be gained from the ability of the organization to exploit differences in capital and product markets, with the intention of transcending learning throughout the firm, and also manage any uncertainty in the economic or political environment in different countries or regions.

Although the mindset of businesses and organizations is that there is high competition everywhere and that the conditions for doing business are unfavorable.

These challenges are grouped into:

- Technical perspective.
- Managerial perspective
- Relationships perspective

They can be further broken down into the following:

Transaction Costs

In the organization, the decision to determine the boundaries to outsourcing business processes and creating a supply chain outside of the organization should be subject to an assessment, which is dependent on where the organizational boundary lies.

Therefore, an economic evaluation is needed to determine the various merits of integration versus market provision. Hence, the decision is based solely on a transaction costs approach, where there is an "examination of the comparative costs of planning, adapting, and monitoring task completion under alternative governance structures."

The decision to outsource is focused mainly on the management of recurring business transactions. The key proportions in this context are; uncertainty in the transaction, and asset specificity relevant to the transaction.

Since these proportions are not constant, there will exist a variety of contexts, and this will result in diversity within the governance structures of the organization.

Strategy and Planning

Strategy theory cannot be separated from supply chain management. If supply chain management is to be regarded as a phenomenon under long-term competitiveness in business operations, strategy and planning cannot be put aside.

An effective supply chain must have two major characteristics, namely; flexibility, and ability to withstand uncertainty. Consequently, if an organization is to attain success in the case of environmental change, then supply chain management should be seen as highly crucial to the adaptation process.

Customer order management

Thee demand from customer is ever-increasing, and they are gradually increasing their expectations, and expecting a higher level of satisfaction in terms of service value. Value chain partners like (suppliers, service providers) can be used to provide a different form of product or service that meet the level of expectations of the customers.

The decisions will in-turn increase profitability and revenue, which is the driving force for customer order management performance.

Though the organization is more profit and revenue aware, it might be a "short-term view," this view may be due to the economic conditions of the market around the world in recent times. But in the long-run, placing more attention on customer satisfaction will initiate a substantial and significant increase in profit and revenue that is generated by the organization.

Logistic Management

Organizations that have multiple platforms, many shareholders, will face colossal supply chain problems, as there will be restraints on operations in the organization. And the more constraints on the supply chain, the more difficult it becomes for a company to decide on what goods to buy, which facilities will the products be stored and processed, what will be the best form of packaging for the processed products, which components they feel should be bought, etc.

Companies that operate multiple platforms, and have numerous stakeholders may face problems of communication. As there will be many departments involved in making these decisions. Therefore, not giving a chance to fluidity or the free flow of information, since there are many parties involved, and this can have a massive effect on profits and revenue that is being generated by the organization.

Manage Operation Flexibility

Flexibility in operations is essential in an organization to be able to balance supply and demand to meet the ever-changing forces of demand globally. The significant challenges to attaining flexibility in operations, any organization can face are; Switching Costs and Coordination Costs.

These obstacles can only be successfully evaded if, there is a global normalization of products and production processes amongst switching cost partners all over the world, which is almost impossible.

For an organization to efficiently manage flexibility in operations, there has to be a well-defined structure put in place for forecasting demands on a global scale and also for planning resources globally.

The best way to this is to do a regional representation so that every parameter in the region is put into consideration. Even though setting up regional representations can be costly and require a lot of personnel, but as opposed to its determinants, setting up regional representations is very advantageous to an organization and will also help in improving profitability and revenue.

Setting Up Standards of Trade

It has become a herculean task for Small and Medium Enterprise (SMEs), and their suppliers to perform business operations. The difficulty in doing business faced by SMEs can be due to the poor state of infrastructure and rules governing the financial supply chain.

The only way out for SMEs is to generate normalized communication protocols to enable the free flow of international electronic information. Although a few SMEs have been able to maneuver and find a way around this, they face high cost of operation and inconsistency in services.

Framework for Analysis

Integration of logistics network steps via investing in collaborating preparation and technology is tedious to set apart or think independently planned location of companies.

Efficient supply chain network needs dynamic organization and expecting ignorantly by strategies will specifically bring about the best in little in the areas of concrete uses for the people involved. It might be worse when it is hindered and remove a competitive advantage.

As a result, the three principles that are the main focus of this research are linked together and interrelated. Examining this area will bring more light to the necessity of any or both.

Chapter 3

Partnerships, Alliances, and Cooperation

Inter-company relation is an excellent boost to supply chain integration. But how do we confirm that statement? The following point will bring the score to the limelight. Let us check it out.

John Champion, who is a consultant and vice president of Kurt Salmon Associates, tells the story of a vendor. He said the vendor invested a great deal of money to design a unique product packaging. But when the vendor paid a visit to the retailer's distribution center, he was met with the unexpected.

What could that be? He discovered that the customer was discarding the boxes away. So what's the point? It is vital to meet and talk before you embark on any decisions.

Another expert also notes the importance of relationships for the excellent management of supply chains. The issue of relationship is more complicated than technological and physical transfer elements.

As a result, it is very vital to understand the relationship, because without a reliable and effective supply chain organizational relationship, any efforts to efficiently manage the flow of information will be futile, and in fact, attempt to maintain materials will not yield success.

Experiences have shown that when a company makes supplier relationship top their scale of preference, they have a better reward. Rewards that include better financial performance and higher customer satisfaction.

Given this, some experts have also figured out that only a small number of companies can leverage their supplier relationships. For instance, companies that actively include their suppliers in the critical business process both in North American and Canadian are lesser than 20%.

But why is that so? One significant reason is the requirement to recognize and involve key strategic suppliers as early as possible so they can set objectives and make room for aligning to business goals.

In transitional supplier, it includes "arm's length" model, which is characterized by multiple suppliers, avoidance of long term devotion, and consistent price reviews. The bargaining power of suppliers makes the justification a necessity. In sharp contrast, the cooperative model lays its attention on the sharing of information, and in some cases, information is shared between organizations, identifying areas of similar interests and mutual competitive advantage.

The cooperative model has also turned out to be a unique element for the efficient implementation of a harsh fast-changing supply chain management environment. Thus, the need for trust and identification of the interdependence of individual aspects of the supply chain as technology implementation connects the gap that exists has buttressed the fact that cooperative strategies are an invaluable tool in the supply chain.

It is essential to understand "common interest" when it comes to having a good understanding of customers. As the customer starts to dictate terms in the marketplace it becomes apparent that the issue of interdependency between members of a supply chain turns crucial. There will also be difficulty in understanding and winning the loyalty and custom of end-users because the competitive environment would have become more volatile.

The survival of the supply chain can be threatened in an environment where inefficient supply chains are identified by traditional "arm's-length" relationships and silo type arrangements.

It is also noteworthy that the inclusion of contact with all supply chain members isn't a one size fit all. To sort out that research was conducted where supply policies and links in the USA, Korea, and Japan have been concluded in these ways:

Since purchasing effectiveness is the ultimate goal of the executives, then, executives must in a strategic way segment their suppliers into strategic partners and durable arms-length suppliers so they can allocate different levels of resources to each group.

The differences that exist between the two types of relationships are defined by the nature of the inputs they provide. The different relationship existing can be defined as managed process links, monitored process link, and not to be mistaken for managed process links and non-member process links. And this is what that assertion was made from.

In most cases, when you integrate and maintain all process links throughout the entire supply chain, it isn't the most appropriate step to take. And going by the fact that drivers for integration vary from process link to process link, therefore, levels of integration must differ from one link to another, and as time passes by.

But there is a key to these levels of relationship. That is the level of management and integration demanded and required, included with highly strategic inputs that demand the highest standards of governance and assimilation by the focal company.

Also, it is essential to monitor the relationship that exists between suppliers and customers with competitors.

But this model gives rise to questions that are worth asking.

- Do they include who manages?
- Who does the coordination and what does he coordinate?
- How can coordination and integration be maintained?

The emphasis tends to be very much on effectively managing and controlling partners, probably at the cost of developing mutually beneficial partnerships.

It has been seen that for some business model, their idea about relationships is rooted in trust. The demand to manage and monitor the varying members of the chain is significantly hindered by the availability of long term mutually beneficial partnerships that are built on lofty levels of trust.

A company using this approach will use the model tagged "managed process links," which will be links that will be self-managing. But how in-depth can we understand the aspect of trust in this regard?

An expert confirms that it is the overall expectancy held by a channel member that the word of the other can be depended upon, which means that one party has confidence in partners' reliability and integrity.

Also, trust can lead directly to stable cooperation, or it can come about the indirect development of commitment. Also, there is a citation of research that indicates a high degree of correlation in the intercompany relationship between trust and cooperation and loyalty.

To identify the vital need for trust and commitment for cooperative partnerships to be developed, a challenge came up, which is:

Since the cooperation is often between members that are either legally separated or have varying rewards, members must realize a substantial benefit from their collaboration.

But the most challenging situation can happen when the benefits pool that some are experiencing is at the detriment of other members. Therefore, balancing these benefits so that all members are often better for their cooperation is the unique challenge facing supply chain managers. But what can be concluded?

From these points explicitly discussed, you can be sure that the integration of supply chain processes can give rise to an effective way of reducing costs, and customer service can overall be improved and enhanced.

You've seen clearly that the formula for integration isn't a simple one. Thus, organizations that have aimed to be part of an extended, integrated supply network, must be ready to provide infrastructure, thereby enabling adequate information flows and streamlined logistics.

A significant component of this infrastructure must be based on robust and quality collaborative arrangements with partners involved in trading. The most efficient of these networks will be those that have the capability of mixing information requirements, collaboration right, physical logistics, thereby presenting shared benefits to a majority of partner organizations.

Chapter 4

Strategy and Planning

In business, the supply chain is a crucial element for development. To foster healthy competition, it is necessary to look into the management of the supply chain and its connection with the concept of strategy and planning.

Flexibility and the ability to weather uncertainties and unforeseen circumstances is a unique attribute of an efficient supply chain. Management of this distribution channel is strategic for organizational growth and achievement of set goals in a transitional system.

Management of customers' requests

It is often presumed that customers are insatiable as their demands are increasing by the day. They look forward to receiving the best form of service delivery, and when this is not provided, they are disappointed.

Different individuals have varying preferences and specifications. It is, therefore, the responsibility of these services providers to meet their expectations in making various products available, as well as top-notch customer service. The major driving force for the management of customers' requests is the desire to make more profits and generate revenue.

The focus on profit generation may be attributed to the state of the economic market in recent times, but this is often a temporary opinion. Customers respond positively to excellent communication and service delivery.

The Customer's response, therefore, helps you retain them, thus increasing your revenue. Subsequently, revenue generation will be dependent on customer-centered approach.

Logistic Management

Management of logistics in the supply chain of companies with different locations can be complicated. It often involves many stakeholders and limitations throughout the business structure.

The complexity of the supply chain makes for difficulty in answering fundamental business questions like the type of crude to be bought, its means of transportation, facilities for processing, the best slate for the product and the decision of parts to be manufactured or purchased.

Various departments in a company such as operations, supply chain, and planning contribute to the decision making process. Relations and interactions between the different groups are often inconsistent and non-transparent because individual groups improve their private sector and objectives, neglecting others. The outcome of this action may take a toll on profits.

Operation flexibility management

Switching costs and Coordination costs are a barrier to operating flexibility. Switching costs can be reduced if all SC partners standardizing their products and processes globally, which is seems to be challenged.

Coordination costs can be significant for the global integration of cross-functional supply chain processes. A well-planned process and forecast is a crucial tool for global coordination among functions.

Regional representation to ensure all relevant input is considered is also essential. A globally integrated process with local representation requires costly resources, information infrastructure, and travel.

Globally integrated information systems are critical to reduce the cost of communications and to make relevant information readily accessible or to reduce coordination costs.

Setting up standards of trade

For SMEs and their suppliers, the high cost of technology is exacerbated by the lack of a widely accepted international electronic information standards governing the financial supply chain. The solution is a standard mechanism for communications protocols, rather than many measures. lots of businesses have tried creating such standards, but there are no absolute and internally uniform open standards now, which is why automating the supply chain is so costly.

Management of Purchases

Every standard manufacturing company engages in the process of purchasing numerous kinds of products from different suppliers in order to progress. The technicality involved in the procurement of these goods come to play in the aspect of proper management of the purchases and building a robust infrastructure for business to foster development and stable financial institutions.

Some of the challenges faced by these procurement organizations were the aspect of skill acquisition, training, and development of human resources or workforce, standard enrollment procedure and retaining employees, including other possible professional offers in other areas aside from the procurement sector. This can be summarized as the process of instituting and managing the entire supply process of the company.

Business integration

The processes involved in business integration do not just happen; it is calculated. However, in making plans towards successful business integration, you should bear in mind that change is constant in the business world; thus, projects may not be accurate.

This results in different requirements and feasible solutions to them. In enterprise architecture, which is the disposition and interrelationship of management, computing systems, and information in an organization, challenges such as human thoughts and behavior often make it difficult to unify individual goals. The desire for rapid change and development also comes to play.

Application Integration

In application integration, Enterprise Resources Planning (ERP) programs through applications designed for business activities function using a similar database for data combination. This makes the ERP system unique.

Integration of these applications makes for unity at the level of business activities. The downside of using the ERP set up is a failure to connect and resolve the differences in the software and the hierarchy of procedures easily.

For successful application integration to occur there must be the simplification of complicated processes for further analysis to enable and establish an interaction. These applications must work in tandem with business procedures.

Adaptation to the extranet system

Before deciding to include the extranet system in your enterprise, be sure to verify the Supply Chain system as well. It can be used as a phone, written record, or a fax machine to avoid total dependence on the automatic SC system. It tends to take a toll on the business processes.

- Challenge of taking action.
- Lack of confidence.
- Inability to embrace change.
- Loss of product's uniqueness that is beyond imitation.
- Additional Responsibility.
- Insecurity.
- Unequal Partner advantage.
- Higher Independences rates
- Adapting to alterations in what we expect

Business process integration

In business, cooperation amongst the various units in the industry helps to attain enhanced performance and service delivery. The process of business integration referred to as value chain coordination, is the aim of administration in contemporary Supply Chain.

Modern innovations in business such as Electronic Commerce (E-Commerce) enables direct linking of the organization's internal affairs with stakeholders for optimum service delivery and performance. Synchronization of the various units in the value series helps for growth and development, in areas like decision making and procedures by any individual or software operative.

Integration in business processes is affected by hitches in technicality, strategy, or operations. Legal and political factors also play a role in this.

Culture and Change

Culture, according to the English Dictionary, is defined as 'Beliefs, values, behavior, and material objects that constitute a people's way of life.' It encompasses customs and knowledge passed down to generations. That is to say that the impact of history and events on the behavior of staff and employees is imminent.

In the Supply Chain, the record of events and relationships both in the organization and with others gives a foundation for successful inter-enterprise relations. Closer interactions between the Supply chains will, in turn, substitute for existing structures and look into existent relationships through old fashioned means.

Supplier competence requirements

In successful supply chain integration, there should be research on customer preferences, to know what they want. This is done to keep everyone in business, including Small and Medium Enterprise(SME) owners who may be affected by customers decrease in suppliers.

This is to prevent doubts and misconception. SME suppliers should focus more on increasing the uniqueness of their products to boost their assets. This entails diverting to activities strange to the supplier. Meaning that the supplier has to be up to date on new trends in his environment and build a better relationship and interaction abilities.

The standard for customer-supplier relationship is performance, quality, and outcome of service rendered; thus, other factors must work towards achieving this. Afterward, distinguishing factors will be of relevance.

Globalization

Globalization and commoditization is an incredible topic in the business world. The forces of globalization and commoditization in our modern world are going at an unprecedented rate. Interestingly, these concepts have developed a challenge for industries to retain and maintain relevance. And that gives rise to several questions like how do we reduce costs and at the same time maintain substantial growth?

Back then, when the industrial revolution began, companies search for new markets, new ways of acquiring labor, and new sources of raw materials. The revolution that occurred during that time was as a result of globalization and companies survived well as they take advantage of economies of scale.

Then, it became apparent to the senior executives that relying on supply chain operations can't itself assure them efficiency. So what they need to do is to integrate supply chain execution, utilize the overall corporate business tactics, and to adopt the supply chain as a means to speed up business transformation.

Data and Information Integration

Information integration is another incredible aspect worthy of mention. It entails the dispersing of information among members of the supply chain. For success to be attained, there must exist a seamless connection with co-workers, partners, and customers.

However, the majority of enterprises today only exchange and store data in text files, XML-based applications, EDI systems, and databases which are in different formats. And frankly speaking, the ability to map in between these different formats is indeed a critical undertaken. Some of which include data types that could have a strong influence on the actions and performance of other members of the supply chain.

So in this case, all the meaning of data details must be well understood, and the same data item must include the same definition spanning across several applications both within and outside the firm. Therefore, to ensure that the integration process is smooth and effortless, data must be of high-quality, which means, it must be timely, relevant, and accurate.

Chapter 5

Strategy Implementation

When analyzing the preparation of business to business e-commerce and integrated supply chain management, some companies in the computer industry are pleasant instances.

Dell and Gateway computer are companies that have proved beyond reasonable doubts that they are distinct in many ways. These companies have succeeded in moving the supply chain management from the area of operations to sustainable competitive advantage.

They make good computers like their other counterparts, but they're different in many ways. Firstly, they can build and deliver a customized PC less than five working days. Also, they were able to differentiate themselves through a unique value chain, increase competition, and increase buyers' and suppliers' bargaining power.

A result of the planning of supply chain integration can be the focus of control of distribution means by a little number of players. When this happens, there will be losers and winners automatically because these channel's suppliers will also be likely united.

When manufacturers find themselves in this situation, they either invest in fragmentation, build a different way of marketing on the internet, partner with successful manufacturers, or use differentiation, and create brand equity. Therefore, it is vital to have a well laid out supply chain strategy.

The goal of strategic supply chain planning is to provide customers with the most profitable and efficient supply chain system in the marketplace. The significant steps for the strategic plan include network simulation and optimization, robust design, and optimization of policy.

Even though it is best to incorporate these steps in the supply chain to make the best planning decision, changing competitive environment makes this very difficult.

However, partnerships with suppliers, great direct relationships with customers, and strategic planning of supply chain elements have helped companies like Dell to survive. For 12 years, Dell has succeeded in creating a 12 billion dollar company as a result of the basic strategic approaches.

By avoiding old approaches like vertical integration, Dell and Gateway have been able to overcome the difficulty involved in the coordination of the supply chain. Instead of controlling the required functions needed to create and deliver a product, both companies instead developed core competence in control and coordination

Also, supply chain management and logistics must be given utmost importance for organizations to achieve competent management and integration of supply chains.

In conclusion, to create another means of sustainable competitive advantage, there's a need for the operation and configuration of supply chain activities and resources.

In many companies, this method may provide them with one of the last means of such opportunity as the standard of the products increases competitive prices, and it becomes hard to identify ways of differentiating them.

The ability of an integrated supply chain to establish a different means of differentiation shows why it is essential for organizations to ensure competence in this area. With this, it's still surprising that the supply chain domain is for a few. However, the reason for this may not be far-fetched when we examine issues that relate to the execution of integrated supply chain management solutions.

Implementation issues

According to experts, the key criterion in implementation is the correct choice of information technology. And the use of third-party providers for both transportation and information management is the option chosen by successful performers.

An expert says that many companies are unsuccessful in implementation because they are unable to agree on terms. He notes that this has been an essential reason for the development and adoption of the standards supporting the supply chain operations reference (SCOR) model (discussed below).

In documenting implementation in a European company, these seven critical success factors are essential:

1. The devoted organization, from the board down
2. Efficient Programme management
3. Concurrent, pre-emptive communications
4. Positive actions and steps to spot and manage critical risks before it turns to be a vital issue.
5. A well-defined and managed Programme baseline, alternated as needed.
6. A sequence of flexible delivery events to retain momentum and a high degree of confidence
7. An actionable, controlled, compliant and assessable set of market benefits

An excellent point was made by Gorley when he said that involvement of the distribution center, that is, in a supply chain improvement program within a DC, in implementation, as well as suppliers and several other stakeholders, has been a factor that's critical to attaining success.

For instance, he further stresses that companies in an active way encourages and motivates the involvement of staff in decision making and thus welcomes input from suppliers to enable the identification of areas where improvements should be made on potential productivity.

To bring about a solution, here is a recommendation on practical things to do which could as well be regarded as a stepping stone for the proper implementation of supply chain management practices both in the paper and pulp industry.

- Start gradual, with a single link with which you can build a good relationship.
- Begin internally with one business process.
- Pay constant attention to long-term, sustainable and cost-productive business improvements that will fortify you and your link

- Invest in staff education and prioritize on buy-in from stakeholders.

There are sternly and impressive evidence that supports these criteria. This evidence springs up system at Lego in Denmark during the use of an advanced planning and scheduling (APS). Well, the three most important lessons one can learn in the case are:

1. Don't exaggerate your ambition. Thus, in a little timing, don't expect rapid results
2. Be sure that alignment between requirement and system functionality is accurate and precise
3. There is a need for critical data accuracy.

But are there issues that need consideration when planning for implementation? Definitely! Parnell, an expert in this field, highlights how vital it is for a business process to support new systems, the essentiality of education in demand management and proper system optimization, and the real demand for performance measures to encourage behavioral change.

For Tyndale, it was identified that three critical elements are needed to be verified and assessed and balanced to enhance the chances of successful implementation. These three crucial elements are value - the relationship between cost and benefits, risk - the rate of success - depending on a time frame for consistent results, and method - the approach upholds by the industry to strike a balance between cost and benefits.

Value can be aptly determined by the need to be realistic about benefits. And what does that mean? It means that one will have a reliable time frame for acquiring a return on investment and being realistic about the size of that ROI.

Attached to this notion of return on investment is the real need to understand the actual and true nature of supply chain costs. Added to it should be internal and opportunity cost, system costs, support costs, real investors' costs, subcontractor cost, and assets cost.

Further, they highly recommend: Mitigating risk by paying attention to short-term projects so that it will be straightforward for them to design action plans, targets, and actual-time horizons for projects that are short term.

Also, implementation in stages will avoid the temptation of working hard for a silver bullet solution. Instead, they will focus attention on basics like data accuracy at the early start.

In concluding it was posited that:

The real value of undertaking a particular work in stages and by segments is best targeted in a wholly counterintuitive maxim: With less, do more. That means, as a firm, strife hard to pour more resources into lesser, more initiatives can be implemented.

Well, it was also discovered that structural issues would have to be identified and accurately addressed before implementation. Take into consideration how E-commerce functions.

They place fresh and new demands on delivery technology, yet it is only on the way the business process has been designed. Currently, the technology aims at forcing organizations to embark on e-commerce before they build a coherent model of the business processes they desire to have.

The demand to own the fundamental business processes right and to avoid improper execution has also been identified as a significant and critical inhibitor of implementation.

Research output from An Anderson Consulting reports has found tremendous barriers to the implementation of advanced technologies and innovative management methods. They include inaccurate data, existing systems infrastructure, and safe business practices.

Due to that, it is effectively vital that one get existing processes right in line with new technologies and methodologies since they highlight the role of planning as well as supporting the adoption of standardized frameworks for effective and correct implementation. On such a structure, the SCOR model is found. What is an explanation on that? Let's proceed.

The need to have the necessary business processes right has also been identified as a significant potential inhibitor of implementation. An Anderson Consulting report has discovered that incorrect data, subsisting infrastructure, and reliable business practices are prevalent to substantial limitations to the implementation of advanced technologies and innovative management methods.

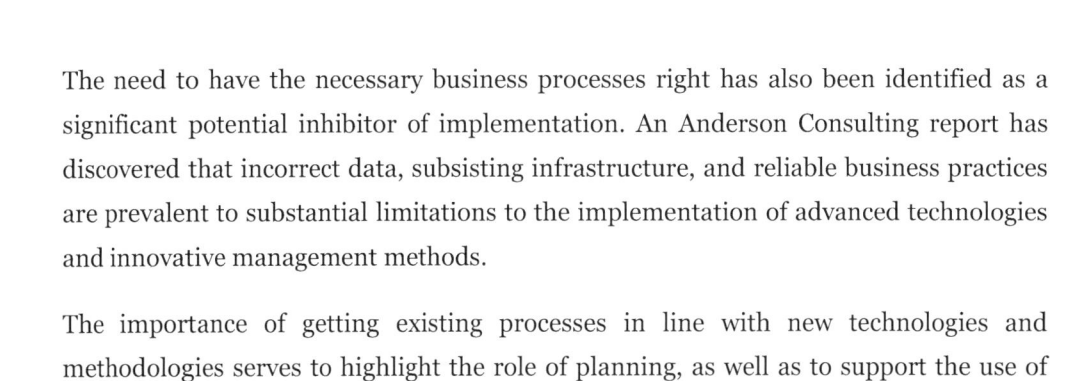

The importance of getting existing processes in line with new technologies and methodologies serves to highlight the role of planning, as well as to support the use of standardized frameworks for implementation. One such frame is the SCOR model.

Chapter 5

Supply Chain Models

SCOR Model

To get a vivid understanding of the idea behind SCOR, let me take you through a little history.

In the mid-1990s, the SCOR model was designed. The initiative was from a cross country consortium of more than 65 countries. The action was dubbed the supply chain council.

SCOR explicitly defines current supply chain management processes and matches these supply chain with the best practice, benchmarked performance measures, and the application of the software.

The primary aim was to develop a generic framework for measuring supply chain performance and ensuring that they identify areas for improvement. Well, let's get more understanding regarding the intent of the SCOR.

It is to develop a business model for effective supply chain management that can be used worldwide regardless of industry or geographical location. Well, the fact is, SCOR isn't meant to be used as a "one size fits all" solution for all who are into businesses.

Instead, it's intended to give organizations a common language to deliberate any issue regarding supply-chain. Also, it involves the development of supply-chain management software.

Further, this model centers around four generic supply chain management functions of planning, manufacturing, purchasing, and distribution. Across these four concepts, information and materials flows are accurately analyzed at three separate levels.

At the first level, which is Level 1, a firm defines its performance targets and gathers the necessary information that is required to build its own SCOR model.

At the second level, the firm develops its own "supply-chain configuration" that takes into consideration assets, product volume and mix, and technology requisite. With this information, an industry can successfully ascertain its expected performance to get to the next level.

At level 3, the firm can work on fine-tuning its performance.

Using this model, a lot of benefits are attached. They include the potential for "strategic" Level improvements in supply chain management via the use of the benchmarking tools.

Also, it ensures that there is the provision of a common platform for communication between trading partners of leverage in the supply chain that enables more effective allocation of resources.

Provision of straightforward standards, processes, and performance measures for the excellent management of a supply chain at the company's level. And finally, it enables more spontaneous development of supply chain management software applications.

Also, even though models like SCOR are active, it is very limited in their application because they fail to model the interface that exists between trading partners, and because they do neglect product development processes.

Supply chain member has also identified that the model, SCOR, is also deficient in some arrears like customer service, asset recovery, maintenance, and repair. With these shortfalls and flaws, we can trace the reason for low levels of implementation that has been reported by those who use it.

However, it must be noted that reputable and large organizations have accepted the guidelines that SCOR provided. And some who have implemented it into their business model has seen positive results.

Agile vs. Lean

When you hear Agility in business, what comes to your mind? Irrespective of what you might wonder, the ability of a company to become more responsive to the requirements of customers, alternating conditions of competition and increasing levels of environmental turbulence is what Agility in business is all about.

For an organization to be agile, it goes beyond being effective, efficient, lean, ability to add value, quality-driven, customer-focused, proactive, and many more. This subject has created heated debate among knowledgeable folks. Some scholars say that Agility means the ability to utilize market knowledge and a virtual corporation to take advantage of profitable opportunities in a volatile marketplace.

In line with this, the real motive behind Agility is identified to be holistic instead of being functional, and it is more of strategizing rather than tactical importance. Further, the concept has also been expanded beyond the existing traditional boundaries of the individual firm to take into consideration the operations of the supply chain within which the organization functions.

It should come as no surprise that the effectiveness of an organization's response to immediately and spontaneously change market conditions will, in a broader way, be determined by the capabilities of trading partners.

For instance, a manufacturer that has key suppliers and deficient quality and delivery records will have a hard time providing high levels of customer service, in fact, if the business is operating in a stable environment. But what happens when placed in a rapidly changing atmosphere, you can expect nothing more than elimination from the competitive game.

As a result of that, reliability becomes a critical point that can be facilitated by the sharing of timely and accurate information with suppliers. At the tail end of the supply chain, this exact manufacturer will once again have difficulty operating in this kind of environment if distribution channels are unable to respond as a result of physical logistics or information flow related issues.

In this manner, the development of strategies for competing based on agility becomes a needed plan for the management of the total supply chain.

Several factors in a supply chain must be considered to ensure proper Agility. They include the following:

Market sensitivity

This is done via the capturing and transmission of point of sale data.

Creating Virtual Supply Chains

This is based on information instead of basing it on inventory

Process Integration

This entails collaboration between buyers and suppliers developments and others.

Networks

This is confederations of partners linked together as against stand-alone firms.

There is an underlying assumption of this very model. And that is open relations between the supply chain participants, the use of technology in creating connectivity and disseminating information.

Additionally, Agility in individual firms can be significantly affected by the level of complexity in terms of products, management process, brands, and structures.

It is soothing to note that there are several agility providers that will ensure that in a manufacturing firm, the process of achieving Agility is met. These providers include practices, techniques, facilitating capability, tools, and methods.

To ensure accuracy in the results, a research survey was conducted. One thousand companies were a survey, and 12 of them were placed under case studies. What's the conclusion? Practices related to people and organizational issues were both more efficient and essential for manufacturers.

Also, it was figured out that a relatively small percentage of respondents only used the internet, mass-customization, and virtual firms, and in most cases, partially. Selection, integration of suppliers with the actual capabilities, and development are a focal determinant of the ability of a manufacturing firm to make rapid changes.

conclusion was based on the empirical study of purchasing managers in the manufacturing firms.

Also, a conceptual model for the design of agile manufacturing was proposed by some experts. The proposal was based on four primary strategies. They are:

1. Technology
2. Dimension
3. Strategies
4. People

It was also noted that the majority of the literature in this area focuses on strategies or techniques, but there was little or no focus on the integration issues. Again, it was indicated that empirical studies that will be used to test hypotheses based on this particular area were not included.

For both inter-organizational and intra-organizational change, implementation methodologies, and technologies for the correct management of the supply chain is very likely to be accompanied.

And this will manifest itself in several ways and areas of process re-design and in many case the development of entirely new processes.

To help a firm determine the success of any implementation, it must be noted that they must select the right area of focus, and understanding the implications of the application for all the trading partners.

The difficulties and complexities inherent in implementation have yielded the development of frameworks as the SCOR mentioned earlier to enable a flawless process. It is heartwarming to note that evidence suggests that the adoption and implementation of these frameworks are minimal. It must be recalled that when an incremental approach is adopted, positive results will come up over time.

Chapter 6

Elements in the Operational Management Level

Talking of operation management level, it is the level that aims at the synchronous operation of the supply chain. But there is something critical about this, which is how to balance and organize restrictions within each firm and between firms via Integration and coordination. The limits encompass capacity and time, information, and resources.

For a more lucid understanding, the integration in operations level of the supply chain can be aptly explained in two dimensions; they include internal Integration and external integration.

Internal Integration and Collaborative Operation of Within Focal Firm

If you are to pick the first step of operations integration and the basis to the success of supply chain integration, the internal Integration and the function to function Integration that exists between the focal firm is to be picked.

Take, for instance; high internal Integration tends to reach a peak of "collaborative internal operation," with which it can be possible for the whole firm to work like an integrated system that leads to enhanced performance and enhanced inter-departmental effectiveness.

Examples are increased product availability levels, cycle time reduction, enhancement in order-to-delivery lead times, and better in-stock performance.

Furthermore, talking about the foundation of high external Integration, we will pick top external Integration. In the year 2006, Gimenez, Spanish food manufacturers carried out a study that indicates that the peak level of external Integration is obtained by firms which for a very long time, have attained the highest standards of internal Integration between marketing, logistics, and production.

On the other side, for internal Integration, it is process-oriented. Thereby, the firm must ensure that they get past the border of functions to erect flat organization via business process reengineering (BPR) joined with ICT-based enhanced production modes like the manufacturing resources planning (MRPII), enterprise resources planning (ERP), concurrent engineering, and several others.

It's remarkable to note that the basic approach for internal Integration is BPR. It prioritizes on the spontaneous redesign and re-strategizing of the processes involved to attain a top-class improvement in some sophisticated contemporary measures of performance that includes speed, cost, quality, and service.

For effective implementation of BRP, Hammer (1990) explains seven principles governing BPR:

Organize around Outcomes and not tasks

Involve those who utilize the result of the process in the information-processing work right inside the actual work that gives rise to the information:

- Treat geographically disseminated information like they were centralized
- Link Parallel activities instead of integrating their respective results
- Direct the decision point to where the works are carried out
- Design control into the process and capture the information once and ensure it is at the source

Based on these seven principles, fittingly, we can aptly pick a core-functional team as one of the rational reference models for internal Integration. Before a firm thinks of the actual efforts of the new model, the firms must define some mechanisms and several actions that will be used in evaluating and performing close monitoring of the status of collaboration, then, improvement of the initial planning process can be made.

Therefore, when the focal firm is done with the internal Integration, it must ensure that they follow some basic rules to help them execute new business model successfully. These rules are:

Rule 1:

This includes transferring from functional management down to process control. The new model adopted is process-oriented, and the decision point must be placed where the work is performed, as a result of that, response to market and customer will be enhanced via the shortened communication channel and time.

Rule 2:

This involves focusing on systematic philosophy regarding the entire process optimization. It can also mean reengineering and optimizing the business process to get rid of useless activities or non-value-added activities.

However, it is imperative to ensure that each event adds value to customers. It should be noted that all these are positioned on global optimization and not local optimization, and the primary aim is to eliminate the selfish departmentalism and equalitarianism advantages.

Rule 3:

It expected that a flat organization is built. To do that; the process has to be designed first, then the building of the organization based on the procedures are followed. Then finally, the removal of the middle-level managers would be done.

Rule 4:

This is allowing everyone in the team play their part successfully and amazingly. Individuals who will be taking part in the business must obtain a comprehensive qualification and teamwork spirit. Alongside that, the organization must ensure that they invest in building a new mechanism for self-learning.

Rule 5:

This takes into consideration the Integration of business process-oriented to customers and suppliers. As competition starts to be the focal point of businesses today, firms shouldn't only focus their attention on collaboration between internal business processes, but must also ensure the redesigning of the interfaces that exist between the focal firm with its customers and suppliers each time they implement BPR.

Rule 6:

This entails resolving the dispersed business and centralized management utilizing ICT. When a firm is designing and improving the business processes, the firm must ensure that they make the most use of ICT to disperse and process information as far as possible.

They must ensure that they convert sequencing processes to synchronous ones. It doesn't stop there; they must also resolve the conflicts that might exist between centralized management and separated businesses.

Finally, a firm should prioritize on designing the right products with the lowest costs, right amounts at the right time and at the right place, via BPR and Integration of internal core businesses.

Besides, high internal Integration must be put in place to enhance the firm's decision-making ability in a sporadic way so that the firm will be capable of capturing the opportunities and win the competition in the fierce market.

External Collaboration and Collaborative Supply Chain Operation

Apart from internal Integration, another aspect of operational Integration is external Integration. External Integration refers to the cross border functional Integration in the supply chain, which can do well to place customer and supplier processes closer together.

Placed side by side with internal Integration, you will find out that external Integration is a comparatively new, and this basic idea is to integrate logistics of a business with customers and suppliers external logistics of by the excellent collaboration existing between the partners.

A high external integration has some features that include: increased logistics transactions with customers and suppliers, more distinct organizational boundary in between partners in logistics collaboration, expanded logistics collaboration existing between the focal firm with their suppliers and customers. Excellently, external integration makes it possible to carry out supply chain like a real physical entity to gain more powerful competitive advantage.

Furthermore, high external Integration can be subdivided into 'supply chain operation and collaborative supply chain operations' that is based on the level of internal Integration in each firm.

The first one which rarely exists is the high external Integration with low domestic and external Integration, while the second one is the real high integration type based on high internal Integration and high external Integration. For the high-integration supply chain, it functions in the form of a virtual organization, which is like a physical entity with very high competency.

For external Integration, it can be divided into three fundamental parts, which is done according to the partner, along with the material flow. These include supplier integration, customer integration, and distributor integration.

Supplier Integration

Supply integration is an essential part of the operational Integration of the supply chain. It utilizes upstream suppliers and high-integration as one of the keys to enhanced responsiveness in the supply chain.

So, the primary focus must be to pay closer attention to supplier's development and Integration to build a partnership with the suppliers, which will then increase the company's performance or capabilities and meet up with either short term or long term supply needs of buyers.

Let's examine some of the supplier integration.

Objective Setting

The initial step of supplier integration is to make sure that the consistent objectives and strategies are set, thus on that basis, they can then integrate information, resources, and processes to actualize quick responses to customer needs.

The objectives often include:

- Develop a win-win relationship with the supplier, share resources available with each other, and accomplish progressive or continuous improvement (CI) to enable them to win the competitive advantage in the marketplace.
- Control the total cost by quality improvement added with cost management.
- Develop efficient performance measurement to encourage and lead CI, and interact with suppliers on their performance in both an accurate and timely

manner. However, it is apparent to develop standards of suppliers admission for their excellent performance. On that basis, it is vital to carry our strategic sourcing.

- Motivate the suppliers by encouraging the suppliers to be involved in all the core processes and make full use of their technical supports, experiences, and innovations to enhance the capability and competitiveness of the whole chain.

Supplier Evaluation

Usually, to evaluate a supplier, the evaluation must be dependent on delivery cost, technical support, and collaboration, and quality. And this is done to ascertain their relationship with the local firm. And it is being illustrated in this way:

- Quality.

On this, there must be uniformity in the metrics on the capability that supplier's quality management system and material presented. And they must meet the expected and material quality of the focal firm.

- The Metrics

It involves quality PPM and quality effects, which help to provide suppliers with the needed statistical information on their service quality.

- Delivery

Evaluating delivery gives room for getting statistics of suppliers and their capacity to fulfill the orders based on the number of requests and date of delivery. The level of delivery is indicated by PPM (Delivery PPM = amount of defects/amount supplied ×10⁶), which is computed based on early, late delivery or excess delivery amounts.

- Technical support

Supplier's knowledge metrics and how vast they are with technology application to help ascertain if they can adequately support the manufacturing and product development needs of the firm.

Supplier's performances in the area such as product innovations and techniques, the process of delivery and manufacturing process, and warranty are all crucial in the evaluation system.

- Collaboration

In-depth analysis of the concept, communication, attitude, responsiveness, and safety performance of suppliers. Sharing of information is always included in the evaluation field as well as problem-solving, customer requests responsiveness, and business relations.

The collaborative relationship based on performances of supplier can be divided into four, namely.

Partners: refer to suppliers with exceptional top performance, and they play a crucial in focal firm customer's satisfaction.

Key suppliers: Suppliers with production topping the focal firms lowest level and extend towards the world-class level.

Qualified suppliers: Suppliers with performance reaching the focal firms lowest level but remain at a stage with less improvement level.

In questioned suppliers: Suppliers with performance lower than the focal firm's lowest level and may experience rejection from the supplier group.

The lowest level of any field is a significant determinant of the final level final while the cross-functional team evaluates each field's supplier performance.

Feedback and Improvement

After evaluation, performances and feedback will be given by the focal firm. Aside from past information and current performances, other key supplier's status is also represented in the report to inspire supplier's improvement.

Furthermore, it is recommended that suppliers with 50% improvement in a specific field such as delivery and quality could be than the early year can be promoted to the next higher level. For instance, qualified supplier to key supplier, note that you can't upgrade from key supplier to partner. The aim is to encourage the suppliers CI activities.

Relationship Admission

Relationship admission of suppliers has to do with plans and supplier development activities after the supplier relationships have been established through evaluation, feedback, and improvement.

Various development plans are made based on varieties of relationship. For example, the partners can take part in the design of a new product while also bidding for other businesses. Aside from this, they can also join training plans, take part in supplier management meetings, and so on.

Distributor Integration

In the focal firm, the distributors are downstream, and they should be treated with the utmost importance. For so long, manufacturers that are into the production of industrial materials have always been advised to view their distributors as collaborators and give them the necessary support they may need to beat the marketplace competition.

This is because the distributors are known as key informants when it comes to everything that customers want. So, they're in the best position to provide the manufacturers with the necessary information needed for them to produce the right product that will suit the public.

Doing this will ensure that the consumer's needs are met and you'll have a successful product line.

Problems of Distributor Integration

In distributor integration, three significant issues need to be addressed.

The first issue is that the distributors may be skeptical about how being in the system will be of benefit to them. As a result of this, some of these distributors that have more power because they hold the inventory will be angry because they feel their inexperienced partners are using them.

The second issue is that some distributors may not be able to provide relevant information because they rely on other distributors who may also know very little.

The last issue is that problems may arise from the new partnership because of the responsibilities that may come with it. Some distributors may find this unpleasant when these responsibilities are transferred to them.

These issues point to the fact that a lot of efforts and resources needs to be employed by the focal firm to gain these distributors' trust.

The two significant aspects through which the distributor integration can be achieved are discussed below.

The number one aspect is through the sharing of inventories within the coalition of all the distributors and the focal firm to protect the unavailability from emergency orders. Improved list helps to fulfill the emergency orders through the traditional distributor management while the distributor integration can reduce the list when the inventory information is shared amongst all the distributors.

With this, any distributor will be able to determine his stock by checking other people's record. Alternatively, with the help of an advanced information system, distributors are provided with a contract-type duty to trade parts at a unanimous price.

The second aspect is to help in the improvement of every distributor's ability to respond to non-current requirements and expressed skills. Every distributor has the right to shape his skills in various areas of specializations. The best distributor can then be committed to a particular customer requirement, such as Otra.

Customer Integration

Some findings have established that the ability to identify, understand, and satisfy the desires of stakeholders is one of the critical traits of most successful companies. Building a lasting relationship with these stakeholders is essential in the integration of customers into the company's culture.

The customer can be relied upon and integrated into the structure of the company if the relationship is handled well. Below, ways to ensure a lasting relationship has been discussed:

Step 1: Requirements analysis

In a market where every mistake made can leave a burning effect, a company needs to understand the dynamism in the needs of customers efficiently. It is also essential to understand the implied needs of customers and find a solution to satisfy the customer.

There are multiple ways to understand the needs of a customer – dynamic perspective, industrial perspective, and purchase perspective. This is needed to be done to achieve various things such as the determination of the targeted customers based on mutual complement, the compatibility of the customer with the company and the zeal to bring a customer that fits the company's visions.

Step 2: Value positioning.

The core of customer partnership is Value positioning. The ability of a company in establishing a customer value that is durative is the most critical factor for a company to create a lasting customer relationship. The process for creating value includes identification of value, choosing a value, and the supply of value.

The ability to highlight ways of affecting the value a customer gets, understanding the value the customer wants and identifying the value level of other companies adding it to its values assists a company in getting novel breaks of value innovation. From that point, the company can create resources depending on the news breaks.

Step 3: Strategies matching

The competitive strategy, orientation, and resources of the company must be in tandem with the desires of the customer to establish a relationship. Following the breakdown of the business environment and resources, the center company should develop a structure or method that goes along with the chosen value position and the partner's desires.

Step 4: Process improvements

The core company should move its primary business ways into calculated ability to offer worthy products to customers. In other words, a company should promote its focal trading ways and make unique.

Step 5: Partnership maintenance

One crucial way to completely utilize the relationship built with a customer is the careful maintenance of the relationship, combined with strict risk control. The primary tool for ensuring a long-lasting relationship with a customer is through rational partnership innovation coupled with product management.

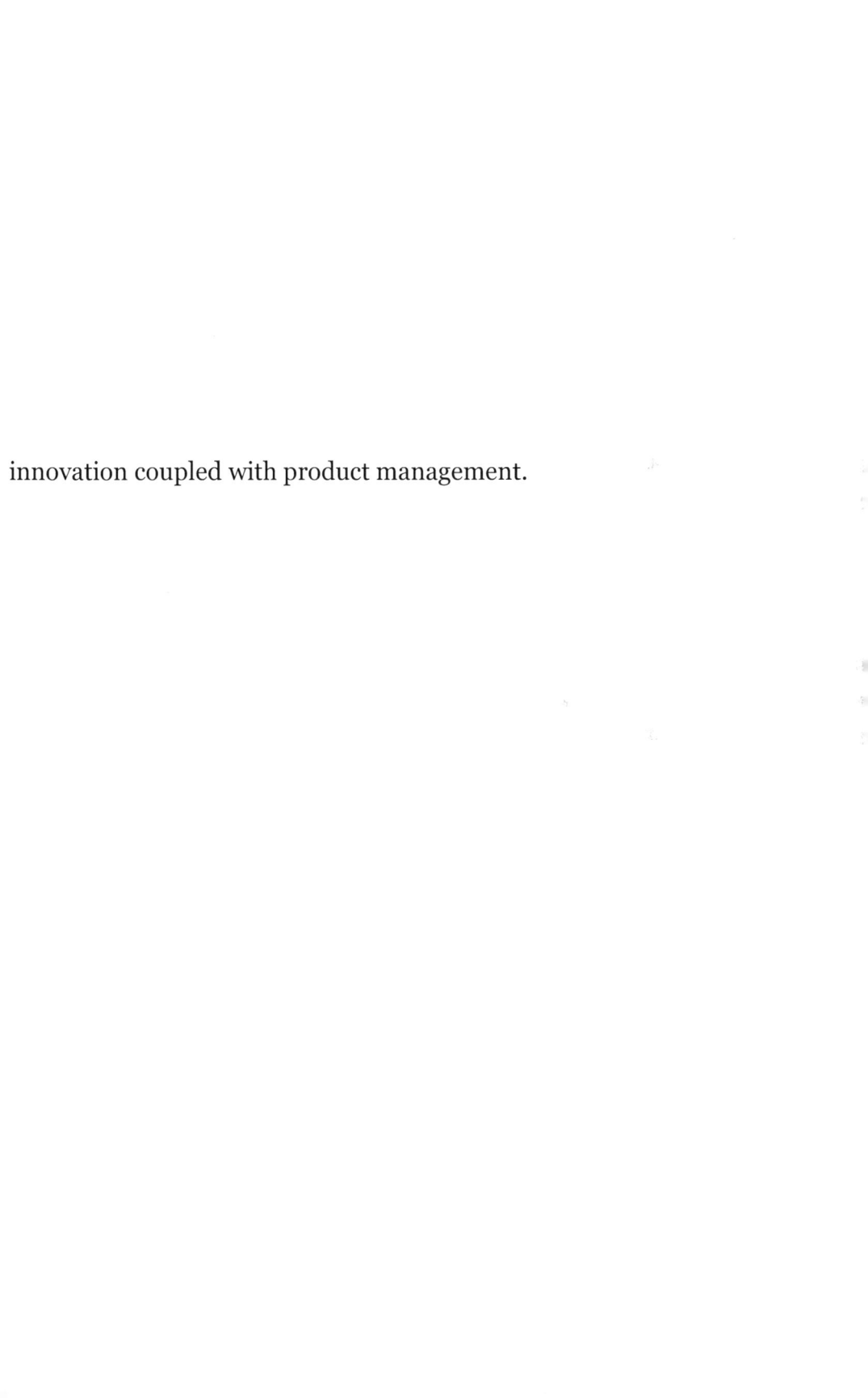

Conclusion

Successful supply chain integration is achievable with the right knowledge and tools in place. I hope your understanding about supply chain has been broadened by reading this book and you are motivated to start off your business on the right ideals and techniques. I wish you successful supply chain integration and ultimately a profitable business.

Made in the USA
Coppell, TX
07 December 2023